MW00619039

Leading
with
Love

Leading with *Love*

The Guide to Becoming a More
Loving and Empowering Leader

JUSTIN ALDRIDGE

Copyright © 2017 by Justin Aldridge

All rights reserved. No part of this publication may be reproduced,
distributed, or transmitted in any form or by any means, including
photocopying, recording, or other electronic or mechanical methods,
without the prior written permission of the publisher, except
in the case of brief quotations embodied in critical reviews and
certain other noncommercial uses permitted by copyright law.

ISBN: 978-1-7336393-0-9

Editing By: Jon Coffey
Front cover design by: Zack Zwicky
Book design by: Brianna Coffey
Photography by: Darcie Waite

Printed and bound in the United States of America
First printing April 2019

4:13 Publications
408 Prattwood Ct.
League City, TX 77573

www.jsaleadership.com

CONTENTS

DEDICATION

Dedicated to my beautiful wife and children:

Jessica, you've always supported and inspired me towards my dreams. You never gave up on me, and were the rock on which I stood to push myself back up from rock bottom. Without you, this would not be possible. I love you more, infinity!

To Charlee and JJ, y'all are the wind at my back each day. It is making the two of you proud, and providing a joy-filled future for you both that inspires me to never give up. Daddy loves you both to the moon and back.

INTRODUCTION

———•———

"Achieving a vision requires motivating and inspiring - keeping people moving in the right direction." - Tom Flick

When we think about leadership, we naturally associate that word with Fortune 500 executives, Silicon Valley geniuses, and savvy politicians. I can honestly say that I have no idea what it's like to occupy any of those positions, yet I've still been told my entire life that I am a "natural born leader." Admittedly, I had the same misconceptions that many people have: the bigger your stage, or level of responsibility, the more of a leader you are. I thought that leadership was all about the platform on which you stood. I also thought that leadership was tied directly to education or accomplishment. If you are someone who doesn't have advanced education, or many years of experience doing something, then surely you wouldn't be seen as a leader in your respective field. If those things were, in fact, the determinants of leadership ability, I was highly unqualified.

Like me, I find that many hold this same fallacy about

their ability to lead. People I've worked with commonly cite upbringing, lack of education, or lack of success in their families as reasons why they would not be a good leader. It's very easy to believe that you aren't cut out to be a leader when you haven't ever seen it modeled well.

The problem with this view of leadership is that the definition is all wrong. I falsely believed that being a leader was a title, but I've learned, through my years as a speaker, entrepreneur, educator, and coach, that leadership is a direct representation of your character more than it is your capability. Leadership is not given with a position, it is not reserved for certain arenas of operation, nor is it exclusive to anyone because of their gender, age, or race. Anyone can be a leader standing on any stage. No level of command or amount of money determines the quality and impact of leadership. Some of the greatest mentors that I've had in my life weren't even paid for the investment that they made in me.

I've been blessed by wonderful men and women, young and old, from various socioeconomic levels who have poured into and invested in me for no other reason than that they believed in me and wanted to help me succeed. To believe in someone comes from the heart, not from the head. Some of the greatest life lessons I've learned and wisdom that has been passed on to me has come from these individuals, but it was their love for me that drove their leadership in my life, not their intellect.

The misconception that money and title determine leadership comes from a simple idea: We associate leadership, with dictatorship. We see the distinguished man who is cold and distant, barking orders and instilling a culture of conformity through fear of consequence. That, my friends, is not leadership.

If you ever have the opportunity to ask someone who leads in this way what the core attributes of a great leader are, one word you'll likely never hear is love. In fact, love would likely be seen as the antithesis of leadership by many. How can one lead effectively, while also loving; that is the question.

So, if you are someone who has viewed yourself as unworthy of being considered a leader or feel as though you are not a very capable leader, then you are in the right place. If you take the principles outlined in this book and implement them into your daily interactions with people, you will find them more eagerly seeking you out, and, more importantly, you will notice that you affect change in the lives of others.

Let's talk about what it looks like to lead with love.

ACCOUNTABILITY
NOT
PERSECUTION

————●————

"Want to breed loyalty in your followers? Forgive them regularly and magnificently." - Jeff Miller

Whether it is in the workforce, a classroom, or in a household, clear expectations and an accountability structure must be set by the leader. When people are unsure of the standard that they will be judged against, they will just do what is comfortable for them. The problem is, what is comfortable for people is often well below what they are capable of doing, and typically doesn't yield any worthwhile results. When the bar that must be reached is made clear, people stretch themselves and grow in order to achieve that level of performance.

Back in my days as a personal trainer and performance coach, I learned about the power of external motivation through accountability. My clients were not achieving the results that I desired for them and I struggled to figure out why. A buddy of mine asked me, "what accountability measures are you using in your training programs?" I said that I didn't have any. After he finished laughing and poking fun at my ignorance, he proceeded to explain to me that accountability is the key to achieving consistent results.

Because I had no system of accountability in place, my clients were only pushing themselves as hard as I pushed. One of the downfalls as a personal trainer, is that while I know my body and limitations very well, knowing those of a client is always a guessing game. Most people don't find great pleasure in pushing themselves to the brink of physical and mental exhaustion like I do when I train. Because of that, even though they have goals they want to achieve, it is much easier to stay within their comfort zone than to get out of it. That's where the accountability piece comes into play. If I wanted my clients to achieve the level of results I believed they were capable of, I had to give them something that was no longer going to allow them to do what was easy, natural, or convenient.

Since that experience as a trainer, whether in the classroom, on the football field, or in the office, I've always been described as a "fiery character." I hold my teams and people to very high expectations, and I am always clear to make known what I expect. Ambiguity is a killer of leadership, so as it pertains to standards and expectations, I do whatever is necessary in order to guarantee that my people know what is expected of them.

For example, at one of my former schools, teachers

were required to post social contracts that spelled out the "rules" of the class between the students and the teacher. I like to write them out by hand rather than recording them digitally, that way they're visible and there is never the excuse of "I didn't know." After we'd established rules that usually shared common threads like "be respectful," "accept others," and "don't be judgmental," I would prominently display the list in the classroom so that I could reference it when situations warranted. If you want to save yourself time and energy (two things all leaders can use more of), do the work in the beginning to spell out your expectations. Once you've done that, you can move on and focus on productivity.

As a leader who strongly believes in expectations and accountability, in addition to general classroom rules, I would also give clarity on a few things. First, I would tell my students that I would help them, but I would not do their work for them. If one of my students came to me with a problem, either academic or personal, I was always willing to walk them through that problem and guide them, but I would not give them the answer. As a leader, one of my primary goals is to create strong-willed, independent people who are confident in making tough decisions in any situation. Because of that desire, I would always leave the part that required commitment to action up to them.

The next thing that I shared with my students was as

long as they showed up, tried their best, and were respectful, then I could live with the end result. In any leadership capacity, these are my keys to success. Whenever someone new comes under my leadership, these are the first three things that I spell out for them. I want people who I can rely on, who will give me maximum effort regardless of the task at hand, and who are guided by respect for their fellow man. Society is quick to place standards and measures on everything that supposedly determines whether someone is "successful" or not, but for me, success is much more subjective. I firmly believe that all other things being equal, those who do these things are more successful than those who do not.

My final core value for my students was that I didn't expect them to do everything the same as me, but I did expect them to work as hard as me. Oftentimes the key differentiator between those who become leaders and those who don't is work ethic. As a former athlete, the mentality of first in, last out resonates in my mind. For you leadership novices, that refers to being the first one getting to work each day, and the last one calling it quits. I don't expect those I lead to be obsessive and neglect other aspects of their lives, however, I do expect that whenever there is something to get done, the amount of work and dedication needed will be provided. I am intolerant to laziness, disrespect, and unwillingness to try.

Along with expectations, as a leader, your

accountability must be spelled out as well. However, a lot of leaders miss the boat here. As the person in charge, the worst thing that you can do is create an environment where your people fear making mistakes. Mistakes are an inevitable part of life and work, but the fear of making them can often be debilitating for people. As a leader, if you create an environment where your people fear mistakes, you will also be creating one where they are not working from a place of passion. Fear is often the cryptonite of success, so you'd do well as an authority figure to help your people deal with and overcome mistakes, rather than allowing them to negatively impact their performance.

Russell H. Ewing, a leadership authority, once said, "A boss creates fear, a leader confidence." When the people under your guidance are made fearful of making mistakes you cease to be an effective leader. Most of us are quick to correct. One thing that we are in a great deficit of is forgiveness. Forgiveness is not lost on loving leaders. In fact, they understand the power that forgiveness holds in forging their bond with those they lead. Jeff Miller, author of 99 Ways to Upgrade Your Life NOW, said it best, in my opinion, when speaking about the power of being a forgiving leader: "Want to breed loyalty in your followers? Forgive them regularly and magnificently." Positive change can radiate throughout an organization, team, or family when a culture of forgiveness is created from the top down.

On the other hand, not understanding how to forgive as a leader, can have significant negative implications. Leaders, live in a perpetually hurried state where there aren't enough hours in the day to accomplish their goals. They're constantly stretching themselves thin to keep a leg up on the competition. Therefore, any hiccup that comes along and slows them down, or derails momentum towards success, often causes an overreaction. Rather than holding people appropriately accountable for their mistakes, the leader persecutes them or writes them off. At least, if they're not a very strong leader, that's what they do.

"A boss creates fear, a leader confidence."

- RUSSELL H. EWING

A loving leader doesn't approach mistakes in the same way. When you lead with love, you don't disregard accountability and discipline. I know that people hear "loving leader" and they immediately think soft and passive, but I can tell you as someone who has had several loving leaders in my life, their discipline was some of the most severe that I've ever faced. I don't mean severe in a physical sense; most of their discipline was of a psychological nature. When you failed one of these men or women, rather than giving you pops or handling it with some other physical means, you knew that you had truly hurt them, which was far worse. The difference between their discipline and that of the weak leader is that the loving leaders disciplined me with the intention of making me better. Bad leaders discipline with the intention of belittlement, discouragement, and contempt.

This contrast between loving leaders and weak leaders makes me recall a few of my former coaches on my high school football team. I'll preface this story by saying that I was always one of the youngest kids in my grade. Because I was so much younger, I was one of the smaller players on nearly all of my sports teams. Although that size difference led to me getting injured quite often because of a little issue I liked to call "big heart, little brain," it had always impacted my drive and determination to be successful on the field. Once I made it to the varsity level, things changed a bit. For the first time in my life, my size, or lack thereof, served to the detriment of my belief that I could be successful.

In my first ever varsity football game, I remember being a nervous wreck all day. The typically quiet, but supremely confident Justin was replaced with a person full of self-doubt. Once the game started, I vividly remember my head coach calling out, "give me a receiver." My wide receivers coach then reached over and grabbed me and said, "Justin, get in there." This particular coach had been working with me for several years at this point, and knew the type of player that I was, which created great rapport. I remember breaking the huddle and running out to my position, only to experience one of the most frightening moments of my athletic career. As all 5'9" and 150 pounds of me took my stance, I was greeted by what sounded like an angry dog standing across from me. I turn my head to see this extremely muscular grown man in football pads inches away literally barking at me. My fear and self-doubt amplified in that moment. The ball was snapped, and the opposing player proceeded to grab the breastplate of my shoulder pads, lift me off the ground, and violently drive me into the turf.

After picking myself and my ego up off the ground, I ran off to the sideline. A few plays later, my head coach called out, "Aldridge, come here." He was ready to send me back in the game with the next play, but I wasn't ready. As he's giving me the play call, I mumbled, "coach, I can't." Now, if you know anything about being an athlete, you know that there are fewer ways to get pulled faster from whatever you are doing than saying "I can't" to your coach. As soon as my coach heard those words roll off my tongue, he immediately burst into a rant that drove what little self-esteem I had remaining from my body. In my entire athletic career, I had never been made to feel more worthless than my coach made me feel that day.

As badly as the things that coach said to and about me hurt, what hurt worse was the disappointed look on the face of my wide receivers coach when he came over and calmly told me that I needed to go sit the rest of the game on the bench. Getting sent to the bench by him hurt more than getting dog cussed by the head coach. That game ended in a massive defeat, which led to a barrage of indirect blows from my head coach such as, "we even had guys who quit in the middle of the damn game." After getting back to our facility and getting ready to head home, I walked out the doors to find my receivers coach waiting for me. He looked me straight in the face and said that he had never been more disappointed in a player that he truly believed in. As he was talking, I remember thinking that I was going to wait for him to finish and tell him that I was quitting. But then something happened. Once he finished telling me why I had disappointed him, he didn't just leave it at that. Before I could get a word in, my coach transitioned into telling me why he believed so much in me. I thought he was reading my mind, because he even said, "don't you even think about quitting, because on Monday we're getting back to work." My coach then gave me a hug and told me to have a good night.

I went home that night highly confused but with a strong lesson about what it looks like to be a loving leader. My head coach never apologized for the things that he said to me, he simply moved on as if they never happened. I went on to have a good season and whenever I did something well, he would compliment me. That led to us being able to coexist, but there was no presence of respect for him on my part and likely not a care in the world on his. For many, that is the nature of their leadership: as long as the results are being achieved, then we will do what is necessary to coexist. They don't care much about the person behind the task, just that the task is getting done.

On the other hand, I got back to school on Monday, and my receivers coach warmly greeted me in the hallway of the field house as if nothing had happened. From that day forward, my coach leaned hard on me, and put me in tough situations. He was there any time that I would start to question myself to empower and remind me that he believed in me. Were it not for his leadership through that time, I wouldn't have kept playing football, nor would I have such a strong confidence in my ability to overcome adversity to this day. My coach held me accountable for my actions, but he made me better because of them.

Anyone who has played sports, has probably experienced both of these types of leaders. When a good, loving coach disciplines, there is always a lesson that accompanies it, allowing you to know what you did wrong, why it was wrong, and why it's important to not make that mistake again. Bad coaches, those that I believe coach for themselves and not their players, scream belittling names at their players, ridiculing them for their mistakes with no explanation of what they did wrong or how to fix it. These leadership dynamics exist in every arena of life, whether in sport, business, parenting, etc. Leaders are to build up, not tear down. But, you can't accomplish growth without accountability for mistakes, And that accountability must be carried out correctly.

Loving leaders understand that a lack of accountability is not a benefit to those who are being led. Patrick Lencioni, a business and team management author and thought leader, said on the topic, "failing to hold someone accountable is ultimately an act of selfishness." When people are not held accountable, they are not forced to grow. Because the heart of leadership is serving others, to not have a system of accountability is essentially to say that you don't care about those that you lead. My coach could have easily let me walk off the field that night, and not have held me accountable for my actions. Had he done so, I would not have grown from that experience. Accountability is viewed as a negative, but it can have great positive effects if used appropriately.

A loving leader doesn't focus on failures alone, like my head coach did, but actually reframes the situation to use that as an opportunity to coach their people. When a leader is able to hold their people appropriately accountable and discipline them for their mistakes with the end result of building them to be better than they were before, they allow their people to know that they can be perfectly imperfect. In other words, as the leader, you allow those that you lead to know that when mistakes happen, there will be discipline, but it's not the end of the world. When the people that we lead know, despite our extremely high expectations, we are realistic and understand that life is going to happen, it allows them to perform from a place a passion, rather than a place of fear.

Love and forgiveness go hand in hand, and are fundamental in successful relationships. Without both, relationships cannot thrive. When you think of accountability, you must start to view it not only as a repercussion for a mistake, but more importantly, as a coaching moment and opportunity for growth. If you want to get the most out of the people you lead, forgiving accountability must become foundational to your leadership style.

Reflection Questions:

Do you make your expectations explicitly known?

_____

_____

What does accountability look like under your leadership?

_____

_____

Are you a forgiving leader?

_____

_____

Is there anyone that you are persecuting for past mistakes?

_____

_____

Do you coach those that you lead through mistakes and failures?

_____

_____

EMPOWER

―――――•――――――

"A sign of a good leader is not how many followers you have, but how many leaders you create." - Ghandi

have had the blessing of serving under both great and not so great leaders. Because of those experiences, I know, firsthand, the impact that leadership has on self-esteem, enjoyment, and desire to be successful. There are many differences between strong and weak leaders, but one of the most glaring differences is in the area of empowerment.

Empowerment, by definition, is the granting of the power, right, or authority to perform various acts or duties. In other words, it is a leader allowing their people the opportunity to do things, and to do them from a place of authority.

A tell-tale sign of a weak leader is one who wants to control everyone and everything, and has to have absolute control of every task that takes place under them. These people are typically power-hungry, egomaniacs who live with the disillusionment that leadership is all about them.

When a task or opportunity arises, their default thought is about how it can benefit them in their pursuit of further success. The problem is, these people have completely lost sight of the true intention of leadership.

I love how Ghandi described leadership, saying "a sign of a good leader is not how many followers you have, but how many leaders you create." A leader must have followers (you can't "lead" no one). But, that fact doesn't make you unique. What differentiates a good leader from a bad one, or I would even argue an actual leader from a fake, is the ability to create new leaders. In other words, great leaders are those who are people-focused, whereas fake ones may be task focused, but are definitely self-focused.

Zig Ziglar, the renowned motivational speaker, once said, "You don't build a business -- you build people -- and then people build the business." Leaders are not supposed to be seeking greater validation by completing the day-to-day tasks with the intent of showing how great they are. Many leaders will analyze every detail of a situation when it arises, come up with a solution, and then begin to delegate out specific tasks that can be done by their people in order to reach that solution. But the problem is this is a weak, task-focused brand of leadership.

"You don't build a business --
you build people -- and then
people build the business."

- ZIG ZIGLAR

When I think back on my early coaching days, I remember how hard it was to focus on the people and not the tasks. It wasn't because I didn't know my stuff, but because I had the same misperception about the purpose of leadership . Because I was so recently removed from being a division I NCAA football player, and still had that ego that helped to make me successful on the field, I still wanted to be in the spotlight. I tried to control every aspect of coaching directly from the sideline, refusing to let my players make decisions on their own. They excelled and did things very well with that approach; except when they didn't. And the problem was, when I made a mistake, they made a mistake. I had created athletic robots who could do exactly what they were programmed to do, but nothing more.

When I left that job, I followed up with my former players, and found out that they were struggling mightily in their new system. It wasn't until later that I figured out why. I had so handicapped those poor young men by not letting them make decisions, fail, learn, and then do it all again in order to grow. As a leader, like many others, I thought that any mistake my players made was a direct reflection of my leadership, and I refused to be painted in a bad light at someone else's expense. So, instead, I controlled every detail myself. That's bad leadership!

When you lead with love, you hone in on the second part of what Ziggler said -- you build people who then build what you desire. Delegation is often seen as a necessary skill for leaders, and in some respects it is, but not on a micro level. As the person in charge, you will always be held liable for the success of those that you lead, but you will not make them more successful by doing their work for them. A loving leader trusts his people, and finds joy in their success; therefore, they allow them to use their strengths to make real, authoritative decisions that will lead to that same end solution. By empowering your people, you take on the role of a coach who puts his people in the position where *they* can succeed the best, rather than a commander who puts his people in the position where *he* can succeed the best.

I'll never forget a former baseball coach of mine, and the lessons he taught me about empowerment. I remember the first time I showed up to a game and he said to me, "Justin, you got the ball today," which meant that I was pitching that game. The problem, and what immediately induced my anxiety, was that I had never pitched. Sensing my apprehension in this, he started explaining to me why

I needed this experience, and how I was going to be better as a result of it. Although I can't say that the anxiety went away, I did leave believing that the experience was in my best interest. Empowerment leaders have that effect. They not only give their people the room to make decisions, they actually push them to do so because they understand the necessity of the growth that will come. That wasn't the only time my baseball coach pushed me like that, and I know I was better because of it.

When a leader is able to humble themselves enough to stop seeking accomplishment through tasks, and start seeking it through the growth of those that they lead, there is a powerful shift that takes place. People who are empowered and trust that they are supported have much greater self-esteem levels, which directly affects their level of success. Empowered people also find much greater joy in whatever it is that they are doing because they begin to feel a sense of shared ownership. So, if you are a business manager with high employee turnover, or a coach with high numbers of athletes quitting, start by making an effort in the way of empowerment, and watch all of that change.

I love what Steve Jobs, the late Apple CEO, said: "It doesn't make any sense to hire smart people and then tell them what to do; we hire smart people so that they can tell us what to do." If you want to be a truly great leader, you must learn to love your people more than you love your ego. You must learn to be people-focused, and stop worrying about the number of followers you have. Instead, focus on empowering the people who currently follow you and how many leaders you are creating.

Reflection Questions:

Are you an empowering leader?

_____

_____

Do you micromanage?

_____

_____

Are you a delegator? If so, is it on a micro level (small meaningless tasks thought out by you) or a macro level (large tasks that grant creative and personal freedom)?

_____

_____

Who's a promising young leader that you can empower?

_____

_____

ENCOURAGE

———•———

"Encouragement is oxygen for the soul. It takes very little effort to give it, but the return in others is huge." - John C. Maxwell

f empowerment is the vehicle that is going to allow you to achieve your greatest goal, which is to create new leaders, then encouragement is the fuel that powers it. Encouragement is the prerequisite to empowerment. Because empowerment is about putting those that you lead in positions that grow and stretch them - positions that are oftentimes uncomfortable - without encouragement, you may leave them feeling overwhelmed. Encouragement, as John C. Maxwell, one of my leadership heroes, describes it in his book *Be A People Person: Effective Leadership Through Effective Relationships,* is about "knowing what gives people courage, what spurs them to action." When you are able to bring out the courage of those that you lead, there is a chain reaction that leads to empowerment, which increases their drive and determination in whatever situation you put them in.

The reason encouragement is so vital to loving leaders

is because we live in a time where our default relational re-action is to tear one another down and discourage. We operate in this hyper-competitive society where our primary focus is gaining at all costs, even if it is at the expense of others. We get excited about the failures of other people, and find it hard to praise and congratulate their successes. It is no wonder the media and entertainment industries are able to captivate audiences by glamorizing this sort of behavior. It has become so commonplace within our society, and so many can relate to it, that people even enjoy watching it on television and in movies.

I have experienced this sort of behavior firsthand throughout my career, as you probably have also. We've all likely seen the person who is so driven toward success, that they view everyone as a means to an end. In my first corporate job, there was a guy my age who fit this bill. Any time someone made an honest mistake, he was the first one to point it out, not to that person, to the managerial team. This guy was very celebratory of the failures of his coworkers, making sarcastic and condescending remarks when one of us would mess up. With the nature of the business, much of our workload consisted of interdependent, team-based projects. Like clockwork, when a new project would start, it didn't take long for him to go rogue on us. The team would thoroughly plan and implement strategies, while he began doing his own thing behind the scenes. Inevitably, shortly into a new project, we would receive an email from him to the big bosses, that we were all tagged in, touting his productivity and brilliance. This guy worked tirelessly every single day with the intention of moving up the ladder at the expense of every one of us.

Unfortunately, this sort of behavior is not only reserved for, or seen at, the lower levels of operation in life. Leaders, in hopes of continuing their pursuits of success, often fall victim to the same mentalities and behaviors.

For leaders, because our success is mostly achieved through the efforts and works of others, it is easy to fall into a pattern of overreacting to failures and underreacting to the successes of those that we lead. To combat these pitfalls, we can use encouragement to uplift, motivate, and inspire, rather than tear down and criticize.

As someone who has served in leadership capacities across a large spectrum of platforms, the necessity of being a strong encourager is not lost on me. I have personally observed the importance of encouragement as it relates to the successes of those that I have lead. At the times where I was not empowering my people through encouragement, their performances suffered and they were more apprehensive when challenged. A great example of this was in my professional communications classes. We all know that public speaking is something that the vast majority of the population doesn't like. My class was no different. It was an anxiety-inducing experience for about 95 percent of my students. Because of that fact, if I did a poor job of encouraging them through their concerns and apprehensions, they typically dreaded the experience, and got no growth out of a class that was pivotal in their relational development and communication skills.

On the contrary, when I actively engaged in a loving, supportive way, I would find them being highly inspired and motivated towards success, and willing to take on new challenges. I would love to say that I am so highly encouraging and inspiring that every one of my students fell in love with public speaking, but we both know that would be a lie. However, even though that wasn't the reality, my encouragement, and the encouragement of their classmates, did have a significant impact. I was able to get kids who struggled to look me in the eyes on the first day of class, to be comfortable standing next to their desks answering questions out loud. In my book, that is a huge win!

Encouragement is so important because it's the way that you strategically grow your people into the students, employees, athletes, or anyone else you want them to be. By encouraging, praising, and rewarding certain behaviors, skills, or attitudes, you are more likely to get those things continuously. So if you are a boss, encouraging the skills that are most important for an employee to excel at a given task will lead to greater successes.

In addition to building success habits through encouragement, we are also able to uplift those we lead through simple acts. We all know that life doesn't stop, and it's not always sunshine and rainbows. Tough things - things like heartbreak, sickness, and death - are inevitably going to happen, and when they do your words of encouragement or small gestures of kindness can go a long way in getting your people through those time. I love, the author, John Holmes' words when he said, "there is no exercise better for the heart than reaching down and lifting people up." Another way that you can breed undying loyalty in your followers is to encourage and uplift them during their greatest times of weakness.

> *"There is no exercise better for the heart than reaching down and lifting people up."*
>
> - JOHN HOLMES

As a leader, and for people in general, it is very easy to underestimate the impact that our words of encouragement have on others. I implore you, please do not give in to this fallacy. Your words are more powerful than you know. To quote Maxwell again, "Encouragement is oxygen for the soul. It takes very little effort to give it, but the return in others is huge." Leaders focus so much of their time on tasks and getting things done, that they forget to slow down enough to encourage their people. What they are failing to realize is that if they were to invest more of their time and effort into this part of their job, it would make the task part so much easier. What I mean is that if encouragement is the fuel to empowerment, by being more encouraging, you are increasing the empowerment of those that you're leading, which will result in them being more productive.

Your ability to both grow and uplift your followers is endless when you lead with a loving heart and a spirit of encouragement.

Reflection Questions:

Are you an encouraging leader?

_____

_____

Who was the most encouraging leader you've had? What did they do that encouraged you?

_____

_____

Do you celebrate and uplift, or tear down?

_____

_____

Reflect on a time that you encouraged someone. How did it make you feel?

_____

_____

BE THE CRO: CHIEF RELATIONSHIP OFFICER

—————•—————

"It comes down to taking care of the people in your program and making them the best that they can be - not giving up on them and never failing to be there for them." - Pete Carroll

I n the words of leadership consultant Terri Klass "leadership success begins with strong relationships." Throughout my years of serving in leadership capacities, I've learned what Klass says to be true, that the best leaders are those who invest in their people first and foremost.

I understand that there have been many leaders who have not led in a loving way, yet they have still been highly successful. When we think of people like Donald Trump, Nick Saban, or Oprah, there is no questioning the the abundance of success that these individuals have had throughout their lives and career. But, success is subjective. Because we live in a materialistic, financially-driven society, success is typically measured by money made or awards received.

*"Leadership success begins
with strong relationships."*

- TERRI KLASS

I will never have the audacity to say that those things flat out aren't important, but when you lead with love you understand that those things are gained, not by yourself, but with the help from others. Success, by a loving leader's standards, can include those things, but is built around the relational aspect of what they do. That understanding further strengthens their appreciation for those that they lead.

If we want to continue to grow as leaders, it's helpful to look back and learn from people who were successful at various points in history. But, I think there are a few factors to consider when thinking about the successes of the leaders of past generations, the first of which is the time in which those leaders led.

The reason Baby Boomers and those of Generation X could lead the way they did, focusing on production over people and in a more autocratic manner, is largely due to the fact that people were less educated and had significantly less employment options.

Today, because of the competition in most career fields and the fact that people have more options, they are unwilling to put up with some dictatorial figure barking order and instilling fear. Nowadays, people are apt to up and quit before they will put up with a bad boss. According to research, the number one reason that people leave their job is because of a bad relationship with their boss. According to that same report, "employees don't need to be friends with their boss, but they need to have a relationship... To have a toxic relationship with the person an employee reports to undermines the employee's engagement, confidence, and commitment." Those same toxic relationships with bad bosses are a primary reason why the average person has twelve job changes during their career. Leaders must understand the direct impact they have on employee satisfaction and commitment, and recognize when they are affecting those things in a negative way because of their leadership style.

In generations past, the person who was the leader was in that role because of their seniority and experience. Very seldomly would you see a situation where the leader was a younger person leading older people. In addition, most of those people never received formal leadership training, and just leaned on their experiences with other leaders to shape their leadership style.

Today though, it is common for great young minds to be leading their older counterparts. Due to the abundance of advanced degrees, not only are people more academically qualified, but students are graduating and going into the workforce with an understanding of relationship strategies and how to appropriately relate to those they lead.

Itzik Amiel, a prominent mind in the areas of leadership and networking, also advocates for strong relationship skills in leaders. When speaking to young leaders he tells them that their number one job title needs to be the CRO, or the Chief Relationship Officer. I know that may sound like a made up position, and in Amiel's explanation it may be, but companies are beginning to actually create this position within their walls, in hopes of furthering the understanding of their people to the importance of building relationships.

According to one job listing I saw, "the Chief Relationship Officer builds and drives the growth of a robust relationship ecosystem for our business." By the time you read this, who knows, CRO may be a common position within the corporate world. But, until that time comes, companies are putting great emphasis on building and maintaining a strong working dynamic among its people, understanding the benefits that come along with it.

Amiel often speaks about how the single greatest determinant of successful leadership is the ability to build and maintain successful relationships. Pete Carroll, head coach of the Seattle Seahawks, echoed that same sentiment when he said, "It comes down to taking care of the people in your program and making them the best that they can be - not giving up on them and never failing to be there for them." Carroll, throughout his career, has always been known as a "players coach," a compliment given to those that allow their players to be uniquely themselves, and take a greater interest in them outside of the work environment. Those who lead with love would definitely be described in the same way. Loving leaders have a genuine care for those that they lead, and desire to see them be successful.

Reflection Questions:

Are you task oriented or people oriented?

_____

_____

Are you a CRO - Chief Relationship Officer?

_____

_____

How can you better invest in building relationships?

_____

_____

EMBRACE YOUR PENGUINS

———◦———

"The symbolism of being labeled a penguin isn't lost on me. All the other bird species could fly - except penguins... I hope they realize that despite the fact that penguins can't fly, they can do something those other birds can't do - penguins can swim." - Chip Gaines

recently read Chip Gaines' book *Capital Gaines: Smart Things I Learned Doing Stupid Stuff*, which I would highly recommend to anyone looking for a fun, insightful read. Chip starts the book by talking about his experiences in elementary school, one in particular that shaped his mentality in life and his leadership style. When he started school, he and his classmates were divided into groups based on their reading levels. Young Chip didn't know his ABC's, let alone how to read, so rather than getting to be an eagle, falcon, or blue jay, Chip got to be a penguin.

Reading those words, I was able to immediately pick up on the not so subtle symbolism, something that did not affect young Chip at all. He went on to talk about the fact that because he has always been an eternal optimist all he ever saw was the positive side of being a penguin. He got to get out of class to go work on his ABC's in the gymnasium, every elementary school boy's paradise, while the rest of his classmates were stuck back in the room reading.

It never even occurred to Chip that there was a downside to being a penguin, but he was aware enough to know that it meant there was something different about him. Chip said something in reference to this whole experience that I thought had great implications for leaders: "The symbolism of being labeled a penguin isn't lost on me. All the other bird species could fly - except penguins... I hope they realize that despite the fact that penguins can't fly, they can do something those other birds can't do - penguins can swim."

The larger point that Gaines is making is that differences should be harnessed instead of mocked. A presence diversity is one of the greatest determinants of success or failure. William Sloane Coffin, a clergyman and long-time peace activist, was such a strong proponent of diversity that he said, "diversity may be the hardest thing for society to live with, and perhaps the most dangerous thing for a society of be without." Coffin made this claim during the height of the civil rights movement. As a white man during that time period, he certainly would have understood the implications of advocating for such a thing as diversity. Yet, despite the possible backlash and scrutiny that he would face, Coffin understood that diversity was of utmost importance, and, therefore, worth fighting for.

Yet, despite our understanding of the importance of

difference and diversity, as leaders, we oftentimes don't embrace it. For whatever the reason, many who lead don't surround themselves with the most highly qualified people, but rather, those they can relate to more easily. These leaders, oftentimes, seek out people they can manipulate into a group think environment. By doing so, leaders are able to ensure they are the ones calling the shots and getting the credit.

> *"Diversity may be the hardest thing for society to live with, and perhaps the most dangerous thing for a society of be without."*
>
> - WILLIAM SLOANE COFFIN

Because leaders are accustomed to being high achievers, we get caught in this headspace that our way of doing things is the best (or only) way to do them. We subconsciously spend our time trying to control and change the way those we lead think about, respond to, and handle things. The problem with leading in this way is that our strengths are not their strengths, and our gifts are not their gifts. Therefore, we may actually be causing our people to underperform by suppressing their gifts and talents.

In their book *Athena Rising*, Dr. Brad Johnson and Dr. David Smith speak to this exact issue. As they urge male leaders to mentor females who are capable of leadership, they talk about a concept that they shorten to "hone, don't clone." Male egotism can run rampant in the leadership ranks. Because of this fact, finding a strong male leader who is willing to mentor a capable female is an issue that Johnson and Smith feel needs attention. There are many qualified female candidates who possess the skills necessary to be strong leaders, yet due to the inability or lack of desire from men in positions of power, women are finding it hard to maximize those skills. In fact, rather than maximizing (honing) the skills and talents of these females, many male leaders are actually replacing (cloning) them with skills more similar to their own.

Dr. Johnson and Dr. Smith believe that we should be honing the skills and talents of those that we lead, rather than trying to clone ourselves. Leaders must be able to embrace and celebrate the differences of those they lead, because that is the way their people will be most successful. In addition to the fact that we should not be seeking to simply clone ourselves because we have different skill sets, we also overlook the fact that just because we are the leader doesn't mean that we don't have weaknesses. By replicating ourselves, we are not only squandering the diverse talents of our people, but we are also passing on our weaknesses.

The fact that different does not mean bad is something that anyone who wants to be a strong leader must believe. As Stephen Covey, author of the bestselling book *The 7 Habits of Highly Effective People* put it, "strength lies in differences, not in similarities." Covey is yet another example of a revered leader who understood the power and necessity of diversity within all aspects of society. In fact, all of the men who have been quoted throughout this chapter built their careers around standing on the platform and advocating for diversity. Notice the power of Covey's words: he didn't simply say that diversity is a good thing. Rather, he attributes diversity to strength. By recognizing and embracing the differences of those we lead, we aren't just bringing in more thoughts, skills, experiences, etc. into the mix, we are actually creating strength. As a leader, who would not want their team to be stronger?

When we lead with love, embracing and celebrating the differences of others is foundational in our daily leadership practices. If you want to be a successful leader, stop trying to create bad, cookie cutter versions of yourself, and do like Chip Gaines' did all those years ago: embrace your penguins.

Reflection Questions:

Who are the penguins, those with unique skill sets, that you lead?

_____

_____

Are you trying to clone yourself, or are you harnessing the talents of others?

_____

_____

How can you better celebrate the differences of others?

_____

_____

VULNERABILITY
IS POWER

———•———

"Vulnerability is not weakness.
And that myth is profoundly
dangerous. Vulnerability is the
birthplace of innovation, creativity,
and change." - Dr. Brené Brown

Growing up, there was an unspoken rule that men didn't cry. Unless you were in excruciating pain, it was a badge of honor to be able to keep it together after a painful fall or football collision that you know would've sent the other boys sobbing for their mommies. On the other hand, however, it was a scar of dishonor to cry if you were scared or sad. If you were caught crying under those circumstances you knew that ridicule by your friends, peers, or teammates was in your immediate future.

In hindsight, as ridiculous as that sounds, those same unrealistic rules became even more amplified in adulthood. In the same culture that tells us that a real man drives a truck, drinks beer, and sexualizes women, men are held to the same expectation that we were as children. Come heartbreak, disease, or death, men are not supposed to show signs of weakness. We're supposed to be the the rock on which everyone can stand and be able to shoulder any load without so much as a whimper.

When it comes to leadership the ridiculousness of these unspoken rules carries over, except, this time men are not alone. Because leadership has traditionally been associated with males, men and women alike are held to the same standards. Society has conditioned us to believe that leaders are to be cold and distant, barking orders at their subordinates. If you want to be a successful leader, by societal standards, you better not even consider letting emotions factor in to your leadership. Using the word "loving" to describe your leadership style would be a curse words of sorts and be viewed as blasphemous to the unwritten code.

Another word that most traditionalists won't associate with strong leadership is *vulnerability*. To many people, to be vulnerable is to show weakness. This thought process is not only misguided, but is a key differentiator between those that lead with love, and those who do not. To be vulnerable is to expose yourself to potential pain; it is to step out from behind the walls of defense that have been built over a lifetime. To truly love, is to do essentially the same, to expose your heart to the potential of pain and harm. Because those who lead with love genuinely care about their people, they see vulnerability as essential.

Dr. Brené Brown, research professor for the Graduate College of Social Work at the University of Houston and foremost expert on vulnerability, said during her TED Talk, *The Power of Vulnerability,* that "vulnerability is not weakness. And that myth is profoundly dangerous. Vulnerability is the birthplace of innovation, creativity, and change."

When I reflect back on those leaders who had the most profound impact on my life, in addition to being loving leaders, vulnerability was foundational in their leadership. These men debunked all of those myths that started way back in childhood about how men are never to be vulnerable or show emotion. By no means would I describe those men as soft, wimpy, or weak, as some might suspect. . Instead, I would describe them as men of courage, honor, and respect.

When I think of such men, I am reminded of my grandfather. He was a man who I only ever knew to be a kind, gentle soul who would give the shirt off of his back to a complete stranger. I don't recall a single occurrence of him hiding his emotions, and can still remember all the times I'd seen him embrace the full significance of a moment. I observed my grandfather live a life of service and sacrifice to others, including towards my grandmother, who he absolutely adored. He was one of the first men who taught me that the cultural acceptance of men dominating women wasn't okay, and that a real, loving husband "lives to serve his wife."

The older I got, the more I learned about my Papaw. I

learned that this soft-hearted, reserved gentleman made a life of embracing vulnerability. Whether it was accepting a dangerous job as an underwater welder, or rescuing my grandmother and her children from an abusive husband and father, my Papaw willingly put himself in positions to be hurt physically and emotionally for the sake of others. Because he had lived his entire life as a man who embraced and understood the power of vulnerability, he naturally led in the same way. My grandfather was a great man and leader in light of his ability to be vulnerable, not in spite of it.

Like Dr. Brown said, being vulnerable is not weakness, it's power. It takes great courage to allow those you lead to see and experience that side of you. It takes grit and determination to build an emotional wall, but it takes real power to tear it down. Too many leaders have spent a good amount of their time building those walls up -- time that could have been spent investing in, and building, meaningful relationships with their people.

To be clear, I, nor Dr. Brown, am advocating for bearing your soul and creating a hypersensitive, overly emotional workplace environment. When it comes to being vulnerable, you must use discernment as to when, where, and how you should do it. But, the power of allowing people to see the real you is that it helps them to know that you too are imperfect.

There is one man in my life who stands above the rest

as the embodiment of vulnerability as power, and that is Dr. Chad Barrett, or Mr. B as I affectionately refer to him. This is a man who grew up in a rural community, and spent much of his life bailing hay, putting up fences, building barns, and just about any other back-breaking, knuckle-busting form of manual labor that you can imagine. Because of all of those years of working away on the land, he is as strong as a mule with a grip strong enough to test any man's toughness with a handshake.

Despite the rugged and tough exterior, Mr. B has a heart of gold. That same man who has worked endless hours on the farm, is a man of great faith, who has dedicated his life to serving others in the church and in schools. I was blessed to meet Mr. B when I was a thirteen-year-old high school freshman. As the athletic trainer at my school, he had no choice but to get to know me well, seeing as how I was a frequent visitor. Let's just say that at 115 pounds soaking wet, the problem I mentioned earlier of little brain, and a big heart, really took a toll on my body. Despite the thickness of my injury rap sheet, Mr. B was always there to fix me up good as new.

But, even greater than his ability to fix me physically, Mr. B was great at helping me mentally and emotionally. We developed a bond over the first three years of my high school career, and that bond grew even stronger when my father went to prison right before my senior year. Rather than looking forward to prom, graduation, and going to college, I was focused on keeping my mom emotionally okay, helping to pay the bills, and maintaining some semblance of normalcy in my life, all of which took a huge toll on seventeen year-old me. As things got progressively harder and harder, Mr. B leaned in more and more to help me. I'll never forget him telling me that it was okay to cry. He would tell me stories of hardships in his own life that broke him down, and times when he had cried for others. Hearing those things from someone that I knew was tough externally, opened my eyes to the mistruths of vulnerability for the first time. I learned, through his actions, what real manhood and leadership was all about.

What Mr. B did was so much more than normalizing crying, or making me feel okay to do so. He gave me power I had never felt before. Where I previously believed weakness and disgrace lived, I learned was actually the location of my greatest source of power and ability to love others. I learned that it requires more strength to be vulnerable than to not. When you are able to stare down the potential harm and backlash that may come, but still break away that wall of protection, speaks volumes to the heart and character of a person.

Over the past eighteen years, Mr. B and I have grown very close, and he is one of my dearest friends. He has shared in some of the greatest moments in my life including my wedding and my baptism. But, as grateful as I am that he was there to experience those things with me, some of my greatest memories of our times together are when we've been able to shed tears together.

As leaders, we spend so much time trying to make it seem as though we've got it all together, and that nothing fazes us. The problem with hiding our vulnerability is that people know that it's not realistic, and that breeds distrust. Simon Sinek, author and motivational speaker, said, "a leader, first and foremost, is human. Only when we have the strength to show our vulnerability can we truly lead." Ironically, we spend so much time in our leadership roles, dehumanizing ourselves. But, it takes much more courage to invite people into our moments of weakness, than it does to close them out.

"A leader, first and foremost, is human. Only when we have the strength to show our vulnerability can we truly lead."

- SIMON SINEK

Reflection Questions:

Do you view vulnerability as weakness or power?

_____

_____

Can you be more vulnerable as a leader?

_____

_____

Have you had an impactful leader in your life that you previously mistook for being weak?

_____

_____

Are you breeding distrust in those that you lead by hiding your vulnerability?

_____

_____

A LITTLE MORE
GIVE-A-DAMN

"As long as you are being true to yourself, you will always find happiness" - Amber Riley

Growing up, I was known as a "goody two shoes" among my siblings and social circles. People gave me flack for it all the time, and I never really fit in with any one group. I was too athletic to fit in with the "nerds," but, because I was very studious, I also did not fit in with the "jocks." Therefore, throughout my adolescent years, I didn't feel accepted by any of the predominant social groups, and spent much of my time in isolation.

Because I wanted that social engagement in my life, quotes like "as long as you are being true to yourself, you will always find happiness" from Amber Riley didn't resonate with me at that time, and I began trying to be who I thought everyone else wanted me to be, in order to fit in. Although I never let anyone convince me to do anything bad, changing myself in an effort to fit in created a vicious cycle of doing things to make others happy.

Oftentimes, this came at the expense of *my* happiness. My childhood years were defined by "kill them with kindness" attempts, where I hoped that by being overly nice to people and doing kind deeds, I would earn favor in their eyes. Unfortunately, it didn't pan out that way.

Another area of life where I found myself struggling to find solid footing was in the dating world. Because I was a kid with a strong moral compass, I could never understand girls who were attracted to bad boys who treated them like crap. While many of the guys I knew were out cheating on their girlfriends and being downright hateful toward them, I was the hopeless romantic who wanted to sweep the young ladies off their feet, and treat them like I thought they deserved to be treated. I fell hard every single time, and ultimately crashed hard every single time. Most of them ended with some variation of the same speech, saying something along the lines of "you're such a great guy, but I'm just not ready for someone like you yet."

During our dating years, even my eventual wife, whom I love dearly, used those very lines on me a few times. After the second time that she broke up with me (I told you, *hopeless* romantic!), I remember having a conversation with my dad that transformed the way that I approached my day-to-day life and relationships. One aside worth mentioning at this point, is that I have always been completely different than all of the other men in my family in the way that I live each day, my attitudes, and the way that I relate to people. Not that my dad and brothers are bad, I am just completely different; I was always shy and quiet while they were more boisterous, and I am an academic while they are the social butterfly, night owl type. On that memorable evening, my dad came to me as I was sulking in the devastation of yet another break-up, and said, "Son, you have such a big heart, and sometimes you probably care too much. You need to have a little less give-a-damn about you."

When I first heard those words, I wasn't completely sure what my dad meant. I couldn't understand how people lived that way, and how they didn't care about others as much a I did. That conversation stuck with me though and caused me to take a look around at how others lived their lives in relationship and community.

Against my better judgment, I decided to give my dad's advice a try. Over the next few months, I experienced things that I had never experienced before. I dove head first into creating this new, *less give-a-damn* version of myself, and it seemed to actually work. My dad was correct: I wasn't getting hurt and taken advantage of anymore. The problem was that I was the one now doing those things to others. I heard things over those few months that I had never heard before, things like "you've changed," "I miss the old Justin," and "you're a jerk now," or slightly more aggressive versions of them. Now, I understand that on the surface those things don't seem all that harsh or abrasive, but when you've spent your entire life trying to make other people happy, comments like that hit you right in the heart. It wasn't until I started to hear those things from some of my closest friends that I started to question the quality of my dad's advice. As well meaning as he was for not wanting his baby boy to get his heart broken anymore, my dad's advice was completely counterproductive and incorrect.

The lesson that I learned from those few months was that, above all else, we must always be true to ourselves. If only I had taken Amber Riley's advice earlier on. I learned something else from that experience, something that is foundational to me being a loving leader: in order to be a strong leader, I had to care more about people, not less. We have to build the people first. The problem is, we cannot invest in and build those that we lead if we don't genuinely care for them.

Leadership expert Brian Tracy says, "the best leaders have a high consideration factor. They really care about their people." As a leader, Tracy's words resonate with me. I make a conscious effort to consider those that I lead in every decision that I make, and to always keep their best interest in mind. In addition to that, I go to great lengths to make sure that my people know that they are cared for by celebrating them, checking on them, and getting to know them. Caring for your people takes time and energy, but those resources are well spent when you experience the fruits of your labor.

Today's generation, which is more vocal and less loyal than ever, and has more options than ever, must know that you care about them before they are going to be willing to buy in to your leadership. Being able to teach and pass along knowledge are key responsibilities of a leader, and those things don't happen, at least not to the maximum capability, without your people accepting you.

If you want to be a successful leader, I urge you to disregard the advice of my well-meaning dad, and actually have a little more give-a-damn about you.

"The best leaders have a high consideration factor. They really care about their people."

- BRIAN TRACY

Reflection Questions:

Are you changing yourself at the expense of your happiness?

_____

_____

Have you ever, or do you now have a *little less give-a-damn* attitude?

_____

_____

In relation to your peers, do you think that you are naturally more caring or less caring?

_____

_____

How high is your consideration factor for others?

_____

_____

BE A SERVANT
LEADER

———●———

"The servant-leader is servant first." - Robert Greenleaf

As a man of faith, I would be remiss if I didn't reference the greatest example of leadership, Jesus Christ. Many people see Jesus as nothing more than a soft-spoken, meek and mild teacher. But, like I said earlier, leading with love is not about being a pushover who doesn't hold people accountable through discipline. Jesus' life perfectly puts into words what leading with love is all about, and at the core of all of it is servanthood.

Founder of the modern servant leadership movement, Robert Greenleaf, put it plainly, yet perfectly, when he said "the servant-leader is servant first." As obvious as that sounds, it's not as easily done. Being a servant leader isn't simply doing nice things for those you lead, although that is certainly part of it. Servant leadership is about humbling yourself enough to view yourself as being at the bottom of the hierarchy. When you have that mentality, with regards to helping and serving others, that's when you begin to care more about other people than yourself; that's when you begin to lead with love.

Throughout Jesus' life and ministry, he provided us with many great examples of what it means to be a servant leader. One of the most well known examples is when Jesus washes the feet of his disciples prior to the Last Supper, including Judas, the would-be betrayer. That's right, Jesus led with so much love that he humbled himself before the person that would ultimately lead him to being crucified, and lovingly served him during his final hours of life.

Now I understand that Jesus' example is an unrealistic one for us to fulfill. I also understand that many of you reading this may not be Christians. However, Christian or not, there is a powerful lesson that all leaders can glean from Jesus' example. Being a servant leader starts with feeling. You must first have the heart to serve before you can commit to leading. If it isn't in your heart to serve others, no amount of conscious effort, knowledge, or skill is going to matter. You won't be a strong leader. Once your heart is right, only then are the conditions right for you to become a loving leader.

As a lifelong athlete and coach, my mind immediately thinks of this in terms of sports, and the first thing that I think about is the dual-threat quarterback in the NFL. When it comes to these athletes, they possess immense levels of talent and physical gifting, however, there is a proven recipe that works to make them successful, and one that leads to failure. When one of these rare talents graces the professional gridiron, history has shown that their individual success, and ultimately the success of their team, is dependent upon their commitment to being a passer first and runner second. The problem is, most of these players have been accustomed to being the best athlete on the field for their entire athletic careers, so humbling themselves to make this change is something that few can do effectively.

The player who has a team-first mentality is the one who makes the transition most easily because he cares to serve the needs of those he leads before his own. The player who lacks enough humility to check his ego at the door is more likely to create problems and become the source of frustration for everyone around him. As I said earlier, most leaders think that leadership is about them!

Simply serving the needs of those that you lead is not enough to be a loving leader. True servant leaders are proactive in seeking out these needs, and fulfilling them before they are requested. John C. Maxwell writes extensively about servant leadership in his book, *Developing the Leader Within You 2.0*, and says that many leaders have the mentality of sitting and waiting for people to come and ask them something, rather than being proactive. Maxwell writes, "here's a thought: instead of leaving the door open, go out of the door to where your people are and look for what they need. Then give it to them before they even ask." Think back through all of the leaders that you've had throughout your life, and try to recall how many of them led in this way. My assumption is that your list is going to be very short.

> *"Here's a thought: instead of leaving the door open, go out of the door to where your people are and look for what they need. Then give it to them before they even ask."*
>
> - JOHN C. MAXWELL

Loving leaders understand that in order to constantly and consistently serve, they must continue to grow and develop. Going back to Maxwell, he said "to bring out the best in others, I first have to bring out the best in me. I cannot give what I don't have." One area where leaders fail is that they stop developing, feeling as though they've reached the pinnacle. Other leaders fail themselves, and those they lead, by growing in the wrong ways. I'll say it again, leadership is about those that we lead, therefore, our growth needs to be focused around them and their needs. Whenever you focus your own growth around the needs of those you are leading, you kill two birds with one stone, and everyone grows together.

I want to pause for a moment to look at a few thoughts from some of the greatest servant leaders of all time:

Nelson Mandela: "A leader is like a shepherd... he stays behind the flock, letting the most nimble go out ahead, where upon the others follow, not realizing that all along they are being directed from behind."

Bill Gates: "As we look ahead into the next century, leaders will be those who empower others."

Martin Luther King Jr.: "Everybody can be great... because anybody can serve."

John C. Maxwell: "True leadership must be for the benefit of the followers, not to enrich the leader."

All of these individuals have one thing in common: the understanding that they have reached the level of success they are at because of their investment in other people. When you lead with love, you understand what it means to be a servant leader. Your leadership starts with your heart, not your head.

Reflection Questions:

Do you serve first, or lead first?

_____

_____

Why is it important for leaders to serve first?

_____

_____

Are you proactive in seeking out and fulfilling the needs of those that you lead?

_____

_____

Are you strengthening your leadership by continuing to grow and develop?

_____

_____

BE AUTHENTIC

"Authentic leaders are not afraid to show their emotions, their vulnerability, or connect with their employees." - Kevin Kruse

"Today you are you, that is truer than true. There is no one alive who is youer than you." Those once confusing words from Dr. Seuss, are now part of my personal mantra. I spent so much of my life idolizing and wishing to be someone else, not realizing that the absolute best thing that I could be was 100 percent me!

If there is a most important principle or tenant to being a loving leader, it is the need for authenticity. The reason being authentic is so important, is because without it, none of the other things matter. Leadership expert Kevin Kruse says that, "Authentic leaders are not afraid to show their emotions, their vulnerability, or connect with their employees."

For me, the reason that authenticity is so important is because it is the driving force behind the core principle that guides my approach to leadership. Early on in my journey to become a leader, I decided that my goal was always going to be *capturing people's hearts before capturing their heads*. I knew from my experiences teaching, coaching, and mentoring, that in order to gain unguarded access to someone's mind, which has always been my goal as an educator, I had to first get them to trust me. The way I was going to gain that trust, and ultimately be able to teach them, was to first work through their hearts in the way of building relationships. In order to build these relationships, I had to be authentically myself.

"Today you are you, that is truer than true. There is no one alive who is youer than you."

- DR. SEUSS

During my first year as an educator, I received teacher of the year at the high school where I taught. But because I never desired to be a teacher, and honestly didn't think I was very good at it, my immediate response to my boss when he told about the award was, verbatim, "you all must be high or drunk." Now, in retrospect, I understand that wasn't the greatest way to respond to my boss. For some context though, my boss was Mr. B who I mentioned earlier. We had a good laugh about it.

In my defense, I was genuinely curious and confused about why I had received such a distinction. Could someone in their first year teaching a subject, in which their expertise consisted of studying for two months in order to pass the certification test, really be qualified for a designation such as Teacher Of The Year? In order to gain some clarity, I spoke to my students about it, knowing that they would be honest and forthright. Anyone who has a high school aged child, or has worked extensively with them, knows that they are brutally honest, and more insightful than we want to give them credit for.

In my conversation with them about being Teacher of the Year, I got some eye opening responses. One young man I taught said, "Coach, you keep it real, and get personal with us, so we want to learn from you," while another said "You put us, as students, before the curriculum, so we want to work hard." A young lady added, "You're less like a typical teacher or coach, and more like a family member who really cares about us."

After reflecting on the wonderful feedback that I received, I realized that they were right. I remember saying during my acceptance presentation that if I was evaluated on my ability or desire to teach the curriculum, they'd probably fire me. It was my ability to build meaningful relationships with students, and get them to believe in themselves, that made me an effective teacher.

I didn't understand it at the time, but after some

reflection, I began to recognize that when they told me that I was "real," they were speaking to my authenticity. Whether it was as a coach, teacher, or mentor, my primary goal was to always build relationships, and because of that, I was always very open and transparent.

It can be an overwhelming to share personal things about yourself, especially when you aren't sure how it will be received, or whether it will diminish your impact in some way. Going back to what I said in the introduction of this book, based on my previous beliefs about leadership, I felt as though I was completely unqualified. I am the child of two high school dropouts, grew up poor for a good majority of my adolescent years, and was by no means a child prodigy of any kind. When people thought of the Aldridge name, characteristics like highly educated, successful, and leader were not commonly used.

Despite those fears, I understood that the only way I could reach those I was leading was to be willing to share about myself. I shared personal stories of struggle and failure with my students, and told them about my impoverished childhood. We would discuss the things that I had to overcome, the areas where I felt I had come up short, and what my goals were. I would let them share in my vulnerabilities with me. Some may read that and feel that what I was doing isn't the role or responsibility of a teacher. I would completely, but politely, disagree with them. I didn't conform to the thought process that I was simply there to educate my students on academic curriculum, but that I could impact their knowledge of real life as well.

Another part of leveraging who you are, is using what you have. One thing that distinguishes me from many other leaders is that I have a bunch of tattoos. Traditionally, tattoos have been viewed as unprofessional or "trashy," which is what I always heard growing up. I'm not sure why, or how, but there was such a negative stigma about tattoos that it was almost as if you not only looked foolish, but you also had a corrupt character in people's eyes. In decades past, you would have never seen a leader in any respectable capacity "desecrating" their bodies in this way. However, because we live in an increasingly creative culture which celebrates people's artistic abilities, tattoos are far less taboo than they used to be for most people. Leaders are no exception. With the influx of young blood in the leadership ranks, combined with people's increased acceptance of tattoos, more leaders are either getting them, or feel like they don't have to hide the ones they have.

Dr. Todd Dewett, who is considered one of the foremost experts on authentic leadership, talks extensively about the topic of tattoos and leadership, and even wrote a book called *Show Your Ink*. He tells one story about going to a speaking engagement where he asked a woman who knew him well for advice. The woman told Dr.

Dewett to take off the jacket he was wearing, which she described as "overpriced and stuffy," and to roll up his sleeves and intentionally show off his tattoos. Dr. Dewett, an award-winning, renowned business educator, admitted to being nervous and skeptical of the advice because he knew that corporate America wasn't accepting of that sort of thing. But the lesson that Dr. Dewett learned was that "people respect real."

For me, my tattoos are an outward expression of my life's journey and the things most important to me. You will see, permanently inked on my skin, reflections of my faith, tributes to my family, and depictions of my triumphs over some of my biggest struggles. Throughout my professional career, I have worked in settings where tattoos are frowned upon and some where they are acceptable. I have had some of the most amazing conversations with total strangers who have complimented me on, or asked me questions about my tattoos. Just like being vulnerable, you have to use discernment when sharing something like this about yourself. But when you do share, when you pull back the curtain a little bit, it will have powerful effects on people's ability to relate to you as a leader. Doing so will accomplish exactly what Dr. Dewett said: it will make you real.

If you haven't noticed, I cannot possibly overstate the importance of being authentic as a leader. It is so important that John Ryan, President and CEO of the Center for

Creative Leadership, said, "unless you're authentic, you're not really leading anyone." Scott Stratten, author of 5 best selling business books, also says "if you're your authentic self, you have no competition." No one can be a better version of you, and trying to be someone else is just living a lie, not to mention very tiring. You are uniquely blessed and wired a certain way, and the only way you will be successful is by being authentically you.

Reflection Questions:

Are you an authentic leader? If not, how can you be more authentic?

_____

_____

Do you take the time to capture the hearts of your people before trying to capture their heads?

_____

_____

What are your tattoos, that significant part of you that makes you who you are, that you're not sharing?

_____

_____

LEAVE A LEGACY

———•———

"Legacy is greater than currency." - Gary Vaynerchuk

Where so many leaders go wrong is that their focus is on building up their personal brand, or padding their bank account. We live in a society where everyone is trying to get rich quick and keep up with the people next door. Because of this endless pursuit, people have their vision so locked in on achieving a certain level of success, they lose sight of what really matters in life -- the mark they leave.

I recall sitting in an Exponential conference, listening to Dave Ferguson, lead pastor of Community Christian Church, talk about a similar topic in the church world. Dave spoke about how the hypercompetitive, dog-eat-dog mentality that exists in the business world has infiltrated churches, changing the way pastors lead. Ferguson spoke about how church leaders have become consumed with building their personal empires, rather than focusing on building the Kingdom of God. Pastors have fallen into the trap of figuring out how to fill their congregations and grow their donations in hopes of becoming the next megachurch. With the mission of "mobilizing God's people, God's way," Dave and the people of Exponential are dedicated to refocusing churches on leaving a legacy -- God's legacy -- rather than building their own empires.

Gary Vaynerchuk, the brash serial entrepreneur and speaker, says "Legacy is greater than currency." I wholeheartedly agree. He, like many of the other amazing leaders that I've referenced, believes that life and leadership are about building meaningful relationships. Those relationships, and your investment in them, is what allows your legacy to live on. Vaynerchuk often says, "Please think about your legacy, because you're writing it every day." The truth in those words is something I always strived to get my students to understand.

"Please think about your legacy, because you're writing it every day."

- GARY VAYNERCHUK

One project that every student who ever sat in my class completed was the creation of a goal board. For this activity they had to think about their short term and long term goals. I came up with this project after having numerous conversations with my students and athletes in which I realized that they had never put any significant thought or effort into what their life goals were. I would frustrate students when they would come up to me with a hurried list that I could immediately tell had no significance behind it, because they knew the first word out of my mouth was going to be "Why?" I expected them to have a legitimate reason behind why they wanted to accomplish those things. I would always tell them that goals are the roadmaps for our lives, without them, we're aimlessly drifting about. Whatever you want your legacy to be, you have to know where you're heading in order to get there.

After spending weeks on this one project, all of my students shared their goal boards with the rest of the class. Once they finished sharing theirs, I would share with them what my goals are. During that presentation, I would always reveal to them that my number one goal in life is to leave a legacy. Inevitably, I would get several students asking what I meant by that. My explanation was always the same: when I die, I want people to miss me.

Now I know some of you are reading this thinking to yourself, this guy used the expanse of this book up to this point talking about how the key to leadership is focusing on others, yet now he says his main goal is for people to miss him. Before you start to think that I am some self-righteous, walking contradiction, let's talk about what a legacy is.

A legacy is defined as something handed down from one generation to the next. I love how Peter Strople, a top strategic advisor, describes it saying, "Legacy is not leaving something for people, it's leaving something in people." Legacies impact people on a deeper level; they create significant change in the lives of others. When someone of great wealth passes away, only leaving their material possessions behind, they are eventually forgotten. But when someone leaves a legacy, regardless of their materialistic wealth accumulation, their name lives on. Someone can spend your money and forget where it came from, but they can't unlearn your teachings or unfeel your love for them.

My wife's great grandmother, Mamakiki, is a wonderful example of this point. Though not overly successful by societal terms, with regards to her material wealth, she was an amazing woman of love. Although I only knew her for a few short years, from the time I did, she imparted her love on me. When she passed, the outpouring of condolences and grieving was mind blowing to me. I was not accustomed to seeing people who lived ordinary lives make an extraordinary impact. To this day, the impact that she created in the lives of so many is celebrated during the *Legacy of Love* weekend the family puts together. It would not have mattered what things she left behind, her legacy, one of uncommon love, would have superseded any material item.

I don't desire to hand down money or property nearly

as much as I desire to hand down a lifetime of lessons and experiences that have bettered the lives of others. When I say that I want people to miss me when I'm gone, I mean that I want to know that I dedicated my life to the service of others -- service that bettered their lives. I want people to talk about me, and the impact that I had, because as Oscar Wilde, the iconic poet and playwright said, "there is only one thing in the world worse than being talked about, and that is not being talked about." Truly great leaders invest so much of themselves in others that their impact never ceases to be felt, and they are talked about throughout the generations. I want to leave a legacy like that.

When I'm gone, I want my closest family members and complete strangers to talk about me in the same way: as a man who used his gifts and abilities to serve other people; as a man who made everyone around him better; as a man who led with love.

Reflection Questions:

What do you value more, legacy or currency?

_____

_____

Are you writing your legacy everyday, or just going through the motions?

_____

_____

What's your biggest goal in life?

_____

_____

Are you living your life to leave things for people, or in people?

_____

_____

When you're gone, will people talk about you?

_____

_____

CONCLUSION

One truth that I have come to understand more and more deeply the older I get is that the essence of life truly is building and maintaining significant relationships. I hate to be cliché, but you really can't take anything with you when you die. Because of that fact, the heart of this book is understanding that the ultimate goal of leadership is, or at least should be, leaving that long-lasting legacy described in the last chapter.

What I don't want you to walk away from this book thinking is that this is the only, or most successful, way to lead for everyone. It's not. As I stated earlier, if you are a successful leader who is generating results and are happy with your relational status with those that you lead, by all means, feel free to disregard these thoughts.

However, it is very likely that a leader who is successful, meaning they are generating results while also building strong relationships with their followers, is already doing many of the things listed in this book. I'll be the first to admit that this book isn't revolutionary. If you've ever taken leadership courses, you've likely been exposed to some of these concepts. And even if you haven't had formal leadership education or training, you have probably observed them in varying degrees in the leaders you've had in your life.

Rather than reinvent the wheel, I wanted to provide a resource for young leaders, or those struggling with their leadership practices, in order to help them become more confident and capable. These practices have withstood the test of time, and are staples of the leadership styles employed by many of most influential people in the world. The individuals who have been quoted throughout this book have made a significant impact on the lives of millions of people. If you were to dive in and engage these folks, what you would find is that love is the primary principle that drives everything that they do from a leadership perspective.

As I mentioned earlier, there are many misperceptions about what leadership is, and what makes a leader successful. A primary reason the leaders mentioned in this text have been successful, despite their many differences, is their ability to change their perspective on leadership and focus on the things other leaders do not. Pastor Robert Clancy's powerful words perfectly described how a loving leader views their role and responsibility to those they lead. Clancy said, "Great leaders may be found at the top of a mountain looking back upon their challenges, but the

greatest leaders are often found at the foot of that mountain still helping others reach that summit."

I wanted to provide an engaging resource that would
challenge you on your current leadership skills and capabilities and make you question where you have room
to grow. Much to the chagrin of the typical modern day
leader, I want to take you from the top of the mountain
back down to the bottom. Leadership is not in a position,
or something that you simply achieve, but is an ongoing
process that requires continuous reflection and growth.

One last thing to mention is that while these practices
are easy to implement, they are difficult to master. I'll
say it again, as leaders, we are accustomed to being high
achievers. The problem is, most of that achievement is at-
tributable to our intellect. Leading with love isn't! Leading
this way is going to be a test of your EQ - your emotional
intelligence. According to Howard Gardner, a Harvard
psychology theorist, "EQ is the level of your ability to
understand other people, what motivates them and how
to work cooperatively with them." In one of his articles,
Gardner said, "For most people, emotional intelligence
(EQ) is more important than one's intelligence (IQ) in
attaining success in their lives and careers."

This is all a fancy way to say that in today's world, if
you want to be successful in a leadership capacity, you
have to lead with the heart. Leading with love goes against
our default, high achievement nature because it makes

us tap in to a resource that we're not used to using when wearing our leader hat. My challenge to you is that you will buy in to these practices and allow the power of the heart to transform your leadership. If you do, you will notice a marked increased in your ability to capture your people's hearts, which will gain you that unguarded access to influence their minds and performance.

So, how are you feeling? Motivated and empowered? Confident and capable? Maybe a little worried or afraid?

Good. All of those feelings are perfectly natural, and honestly, essential. No one becomes a great leader overnight. You've never heard someone who led for a short period of time be referred to as a great leader. Leadership is about consistency over the long haul. Leadership is a skill, and like any other skill, the mastery of it takes time. There will be times that you will fail! Take that fact to the bank. But the great leaders quoted throughout this book, became great by failing, learning their lessons, making changes, and moving forward again.

I pray that this book may aid you in your journey to becoming the most loving and empowering version of yourself. When you embody that mentality, you will naturally become a loving, servant-hearted leader.

My friend, as you journey to lead with love I wish you well. Always remember that life is precious, with no knowledge of when it will end, so live it now!

ABOUT THE AUTHOR

Justin Aldridge is an organizational consultant for school administrators and business leaders on creating a maximum performance environment. Justin's focus helps students and employees realize how to truly engage in leadership regardless of their past.

As the child of two high school dropouts and growing up in poverty where he was exposed to drugs, violence, and murder, Justin decided not to let his environment define him.

Justin became a first-generation college student who graduated in the top one percent of his class of 50,000 students at the University of Texas while playing Division I football.

As a speaker and success coach, Justin explains how to truly utilize leadership to overcome life's greatest obstacles. His message has taken him across the country speaking to schools and organizations. As a frequently published columnist on leadership and personal development, Justin writes about practical steps to becoming a more loving and empowering leader.

For more about Justin, follow him
on social media, or visit:

jsaleadership.com

ACKNOWLEDGMENTS

I want to start by thanking God for the blessing of being able to accomplish a lifelong goal of writing a book. Growing up in the circumstances that I did, there were many times where I felt like my dreams were too big for my capabilities. It wasn't until I came to know a relationship with Christ that I truly began to believe that I was meant for more than what I had been settling for.

The original cornerstone in my life was my parents. Although life was not always easy, they've always been there for me, and have loved me unconditionally. Being in your early 20's with five children would be enough to drive anyone to make some bad choices, but they always stuck together and did the best they could to provide the best life possible for us kids. Mom and dad, I'm truly thankful for your support and always encouraging me to dream bigger than I ever thought possible. Because of the two of you, I now know that I am capable of more than I give myself credit for. I love you both unconditionally.

I want to thank my siblings for their support as well. Being so close in age felt like a curse at times during our childhood, but looking back now, I wouldn't have wanted it any other way. Despite their flaws, just like mine, my brothers and sister are my best friends, and there's no other people I would choose to do life with.

Dr. Chad Barrett (Mr. B to me) is another person I must thank. This man transformed my life, helping me grow from a rough and tumble, hot-headed 13 year old boy into the man that I am today. I know wholeheartedly, were it not for God sending him into my life I'd not be the father, husband, or man of God that I have become. Mr. B is the real life inspiration behind this book. Until I had met and grown in brotherhood with him, I had never personally experienced what it looked like to lead with love. I hope that as I grow older, I can be the example for others that he has been for me.

And to my in-laws, thank you for loving me as one of your own, and loving me back from the depths of personal hell. I was once told that God sends people into our lives for a reason, a season, or a lifetime, and I am certainly glad that he chose lifetime for all of you.

There are so many others that I could thank, but not enough pages to do so. For anyone and everyone who has ever supported me, encouraged me, stuck by my side, kept me in line, and loved me, I thank you from the bottom of my heart. While I mentioned only a few specific people here, just know that you all mean the world to me.

REFERENCES

Anderson, R. (2008) *The Executive Calling: Corporate Success Without Selling Your Soul.* (1st Edition) Lake Mary, FL: Creation House.

Brown, B. (2012) *Vulnerability is the birthplace of innovation, creativity, and change: Brené Brown at TED2012.* Accessed January 5 2019 through https://blog.ted.com/vulnerability-is-the-birthplace-of-innovation-creativity-and-change-brene-brown-at-ted2012/.

Carroll, P. (s.d.) *WIN FOREVER! WHAT CAN BUSINESS LEADERS LEARN FROM SEAHAWKS COACH PETE CARROLL?* Accessed January 4 2019 through https://kallesgroup.com/win-forever-can-business-leaders-learn-seahawks-coach-pete-carroll/.

Coffin Jr., W.S. (2019) *Diversity Quotes.* Accessed February 5 2019 through https://www.thoughtco.com/diversity-quotes-and-sayings-2832777.

Covey, S. (1989) *The 7 Habits of Highly Effective People.* New York, NY: Free Press.

Dewett, T. (2014) *SHOW YOUR INK: Stories About Leadership and Life.* (1st edition) Houston, TX: TVA Incorporated.

Ryan, J. (s.d.) *Maximize Your Leadership Success in 5 Ways.* Accessed January 8 2019 through https://www.ccl.org/open-enrollment-programs/leadership-at-the-peak/maximize-leadership-success-5-ways/.

Ewing, R.H. (s.d.) *A Boss Creates Fear, A Leader Confidence. A Boss Fixes Blame.* Accessed December 5 2018 through http://wgo.company/a-boss-creates-fear-a-leader-confidence-a-boss-fixes-blame-p430-204.html.

Gaines, C. (2017) *Capital Gaines: Smart Things I Learned Doing Stupid Stuff.* (1ˢᵗ edition) Nashville, TN: W Publishing Group.

Gardner, H. (2018) *What is Emotional Intelligence (EQ)?* Accessed December 3 2019 through https://psychcentral.com/lib/what-is-emotional-intelligence-eq/.

Gates, B. (2013) *What is Leadership?* Accessed January 18 2019 through https://www.forbes.com/sites/kevinkruse/2013/04/09/what-is-leadership/#32c2d23c5b90.

Ghandi, M. (2012) *100 Best Quotes On Leadership.* Accessed November 18 2018 through https://www.forbes.com/sites/kevinkruse/2012/10/16/quotes-on-leadership/#78b791732feb.

Greenleaf, R. (1977) *Servant Leadership— A Journey into the Nature of Legitimate Power and Greatness.* Mahwah, NJ: Paulist Press.

Holmes, J. (s.d.) *There is no exercise better for the heart than reaching down and lifting people up.* Accessed December 5 2018 through https://www.passiton.com/

inspirational-quotes/7235-there-is-no-exercise-better-for-the-heart-than.

Jobs, S. (2018) *Hire Smart People and Let Them Tell You What To Do—Just Like Steve Jobs Did.* Accessed December 3 2018 through https://hackernoon.com/hire-smart-people-and-let-them-tell-you-what-to-do-just-like-steve-jobs-did-c38d92d11213.

Johnson, B. and Smith, D. (2016) *Athena Rising: How and Why Men Should Mentor Women.* (1st edition) New York, NY: Bibliomotion Inc.

King Jr., M.L. (2013) *"Everybody Can Be Great, Because Anybody Can Serve."* Accessed December 12 2018 through https://www.huffingtonpost.com/wayne-meisel/everybody-can-be-great-because-anybody-can-serve_b_2476044.html

Klass, T. (2017) *FIVE CRITICAL LEADERSHIP RELATIONSHIPS.* Accessed December 20 2018 through http://www.terriklassconsulting.com/2017/07/23/five-critical-leadership-relationships/.

Kruse, K. (2013) *Authentic Leadership.* Accessed December 15 2019 through https://www.kevinkruse.com/authentic-leadership/.

Lencioni, P. (s.d.) *Holding Your Staff Accountable.* Accessed November 25 2018 through https://www.ccfcollege.com/holding-your-staff-accountable/.

Mandela, N. (1994) *Long Walk to Freedom: The Autobiography of Nelson Mandela.* (1st edition) Los Angeles: Macdonald Purnell Publishers.

Maxwell, J.C. (2007) *BE A PEOPLE PERSON.* (2 edition) Colorado Springs, CO: David C Cook

Maxwell, J.C. (2017) *Developing the Leader Within You 2.0.* (1st edition) Nashville, TN: HarperCollins

Miller, J. (s.d.) *Forgiveness: A Must-Have for Leaders.* Accessed December 12 2018 through http://theincrementallife.com/forgiveness-a-must-have-for-leaders/.

Riley, A. (s.d.) *Amber Riley Biography.* Accessed December 5 2018 through http://www.teenidols4you.com/bio/Actors/1853/amberriley.html.

Sinek, S. (2018) *The Thing That Will Instantly Increase Your Influence As A Leader.* Accessed December 20 2018 through https://medium.com/swlh/the-thing-that-will-instantly-increase-your-influence-as-a-leader-4aba0652d53b.

Stratten, S. (2014). *Your Authentic Self Has No Competition.* Accessed November 18 2018 through https://www.theartof.com/videos/your-authentic-self-has-no-competition.

Strople, P. (2018) *7 GREAT QUOTES ON LEAVING A LEGACY.* Accessed January 16 2019 through https://billhigh.com/legacy/7-great-quotes-on-leaving-a-legacy/.

Tracy, B. (s.d.) *100+ Most Inspirational Leadership Quotes and Sayings.* Accessed January 12 2019 through https://www.askideas.com/100-most-inspirational-leadership-quotes-and-sayings/2/.

Vaynerchuk, G. (2019) *Legacy is greater than Currency.* Accessed December 29 2018 through http://gary.tumblr.com/post/78887853/legacy-is-greater-than-currency.

Wilde, O. (1980) *The Picture of Dorian Gray.* (1st edition) London, UK: Lippincott's Monthly Magazine.

Ziglar, Z. (s.d.) *You don't build a business.* Accessed November 29 2018 through https://www.ziglar.com/articles/dont-build-business/.

46424791R00068

Made in the USA
Middletown, DE
28 May 2019